GW01396180

LIVING WITH NATURE

House Design
JAVIER BARBA

LIVING WITH NATURE

House Design
JAVIER BARBA

6

BY MICHAEL WEBB

First published in Australia in 1999 by
The Images Publishing Group Pty Ltd
ACN 059 734 431
6 Bastow Place, Mulgrave, Victoria 3170, Australia
Telephone: +(61 3) 9561 5544 Facsimile: +(61 3) 9561 4860
E-mail: books@images.com.au

Copyright © The Images Publishing Group Pty Ltd 1999

All rights reserved. Apart from any fair dealing for the purposes
of private study, research, criticism or review as permitted under
the Copyright Act, no part of this publication may be reproduced,
stored in a retrieval system or transmitted in any form by any
means, electronic, mechanical, photocopying, recording or
otherwise, without the written permission of the publisher.

National Library of Australia Cataloguing-in-Publication Data

Webb, Michael, 1937 – .

Javier Barba : living with nature.

Bibliography.

Includes index.

ISBN 1 86470 051 3.

House Design Series ISSN 1329 0045

1. Barba, Javier. 2. Architecture, Domestic – Designs and plans.
3. Architects. 4. Architecture, Modern – 20th century – Designs
and plans. I. Barba, Javier. II. Title. (Series : House design ; 6).

728.0222

Designed by The Graphic Image Studio Pty Ltd
Mulgrave, Australia

Printed in Hong Kong

CONTENTS

INTRODUCTION

Javier Barba is an architect with a mission: to design simple, ecologically responsible houses for exceptional clients in settings of great natural beauty, and to employ the same approach in multiple housing and other building types. The son and grandson of architect-builders, he has spent most of his life in Barcelona, where he lives in a high-rise apartment with his American wife Pamela, and their two grown-up sons. Lithe, boyishly handsome, and dedicated to his craft, Barba has just turned 50 and his modest practice is taking off. Several of the vacation houses he has built in Catalonia and on Greek islands have won acclaim for the way they seem to grow organically from their sites. Ambitious projects, including an idyllic resort community in Baja California, are currently in development or under construction, and he has secured his first commission in the United States—new cellars for Stag's Leap winery in the Napa Valley of central California.

'Architecture that does not provoke emotion is not good architecture,' says Barba, whose cheerful calm dissipates when he starts discussing buildings and nature. He remembers his father driving him around Barcelona as a small boy and how, even then, he would express strong opinions about architecture. Adjectives like 'incredible,' 'fantastic' and 'terrible' pepper his descriptions of the Mediterranean landscape and how its beauty has been ravaged by greed and stupidity, especially along the Costa Brava. He is a sensualist who wants to wake up to a great view at sunrise, swim in a turquoise sea before breakfast, walk barefoot on warm stones and smell wild thyme. For him, architecture is about shelter: protection from fierce winds, an oasis of shade for an outdoor meal of chilled wine and freshly-caught fish, taking a siesta in a thick-walled room that's naturally cross-ventilated. Inspiration comes from the rural vernacular of rough-edged geometric forms, of smoothly rounded stucco and stones laid with unconscious artistry, of wide porches and deep-set windows, but still more from the land.

As an heir to the pantheistic tradition of the Mediterranean, Barba is chiefly inspired by the spirit of place. 'It is essential to feel the energy of the site and experience its qualities,' he says. 'Before I begin to design, I spend days on the land, sketching and taking photographs, trying to capture its colours and textures, the play of light and the fragrance of the vegetation. You need to recognize the powerful places that are defined by trees and large rocks. When you see a stone, don't take it out or design as though it weren't there.

It's giving you information with which to start the project. This is a lesson I learned while hunting wild mushrooms—they are hard to find so we have to preserve the spots where they grow.'

Barba practices and preaches integrated bioclimatic architecture—which he defines as an approach, not a style—respecting nature and its resources, and providing occupants with the most comfortable and pleasing environment possible. A lot of it is plain common sense—orienting a house to take advantage of a view, pulling in natural light and shutting out strong sun, using the mass of the structure to absorb heat during the day and release it at night, protecting from gales but admitting cool breezes. Barba has burrowed into hillsides, landscaped rooftops, and used quarries and overhanging rocks to shelter his houses, with the goal of reducing energy consumption and blurring the divide between building and landscape. 'All architects should design bioclimatically, because it is the nature of architecture to relate humans to the earth and the sky,' he observes. 'You hope that the more intensely you engage the site, the happier the client will be.'

Making clients happy has been one of Barba's most consistent accomplishments, but, to achieve this, the chemistry has to be right. Typically, a call comes in from a prosperous executive who has purchased a challenging site for a second home, has seen a magazine feature on a Barba house, and wants the architect to do something of the same kind for himself and his family. The pictures serve as a selection device, attracting people with taste and sensitivity who want a house that's a comfortable fit and emotionally satisfying—not an extravaganza to impress their friends. Even so, Barba is cautious. 'When a potential client comes in, I say: I need to know you,' he explains. 'If I don't have a good feeling, if he seems selfish or overly demanding, I don't go ahead. An architect should be like a good actor who can adapt to different roles, but he's not a worker to be bought. He must have the ability, sensitivity and *cojones* to interpret his clients' feelings in a very gentle way. What kind of life do they lead? How can the design complement that, and relax or stimulate them. It's a very slow process—discussing feelings, walking the land, doing sketches, making models. We like to enjoy our work and build a lasting relationship over a long period of time.'

Architecture was in Barba's genes and all around him. As a boy he met Alvar Aalto, Walter Gropius, and Kenzo Tange—master-builders who were friends of his father. In Barcelona, almost every building is engraved with the name of its designer, and architects have traditionally enjoyed high esteem. The city has a rich heritage of medieval and modern buildings, but Barba came of age in the 1960s when Spanish architecture was at a low ebb, and Barcelona was being disfigured by crass new construction and the destruction of its heritage. A rebellious youth who went through 11 different schools, and spent one summer living in a cave on Formentera, he studied architecture at university, but without enthusiasm. Rationalism was the prevailing doctrine, and Aldo Rossi was held up as a model; Barba found the teaching arid, and longed to work hands-on with stone. He learned more about architecture from books and from working 12 years in his father's office, before moving to Menorca for two years to assist Antonio Sintes, an architect and builder who created distinctive work that drew on the island's strong traditions. Barba married, and rented a farmhouse in which to develop his own unrealized designs.

In 1973, he moved back to Barcelona and has worked there ever since, developing housing projects with a friend, Javier Perez de Pulgar, before going independent, but keeping the name of his father's office, BC Estudio. Commissions trickled in, and Barba called on friends to help out as needed to supplement his one assistant and a part-time secretary. 'Temperamentally, I would prefer to stay small and have control over every job, but now I'm trying to create a group who share my ideas,' he says. 'Some people badly want to grow, and very few can afford to concentrate on houses. I enjoy residential work and I make enough money to live. One reason I limit myself is so that I can spend as much time as possible on the construction site. Constructing is fundamental for me—that's when I learn what works best.'

Asked about his favourite architects, Barba cites Frank Lloyd Wright for the way he rooted buildings in the site, but claims that he doesn't spend much time looking at what others are doing. He feels it is better to forget what he has seen and to simplify his work. Certain themes recur in his houses, and these include binuclear plans with a shallow entry hall separating living from sleeping areas, simple bedrooms staggered on plan to give each a view and a private patio, indoor-outdoor living rooms, projecting roof planes, and natural stone used in conjunction with earth-toned concrete. A circular canopy, introduced to shade a dining terrace on one house, was employed on a larger scale in two later jobs. Many of these features are determined by the Mediterranean climate, and the owners' desires to escape the routines of the city and live in touch with nature. Most have children who spend all day outdoors, but need places to play and rest while their parents entertain. For Barba, space and light are the essential qualities, a feeling of being unconfined and unpretentious. The houses have to be easy to build and maintain. Barcelona families often spend every weekend at their country place, northerners head south for just a few weeks in summer, but this pattern may change as more people work in cyberspace and can choose to live wherever they want.

Over his 25 years of practice, Barba feels he has come a long way. 'Early on, I didn't have the strength of experience to win over clients,' he says. 'Now I have a body of work that demonstrates my ideas and that makes it easier to argue for a logical solution. I show a client images to illustrate my references, and encourage him to do the same—the way little kids swap items from their collections. It helps us select from many possibilities. Also, I've learned how to relax and

become more secure. Eight years ago I suffered when I started a project. I had so many ideas that they were getting in each other's way. I was blocked for weeks at a time before I could start designing. Now I close my eyes, see the house, and begin drawing. It feels much simpler. And, for the last five years we've been working on interiors—previously, I left the shell for owners or their decorators to finish.'

Despite their simplicity, Barba's houses are highly photogenic. Their bold forms and rough surfaces are modelled by the brilliant light, and draw strength from the vistas of sea and hills, trees and rocks. Few see them in their remote or sequestered locations but, when reproduced, each becomes a temptation to someone else who is dreaming of escape but needs to be reassured that his fantasy has a solid foundation. Barba is also a dreamer with his feet firmly planted on the ground, and he provides an instructive model to architects who are inclined to neglect people and the context in pursuit of daring structures and showy effects. The houses described in these pages are timeless and are shaped by need and tradition, not fashion, but they abstract the vernacular rather than mimicking it.

JOVER/RIERA HOUSE

Sant Andreu de Llavaneras, Spain
Design/Completion 1985/1986

1

2

3

This weekend house is located 30 kilometres east of Barcelona, on a steeply sloping site that looks south towards the sea, two kilometres away. A cobbled drive slopes down from the street. Walls of poured concrete undulate around a lawn, and drop like sheer cliffs to the lower garden. Only the slotted chimneys rising from the turf, and a flight of steps cascading down to an entry door indicate that there is a house below. As you descend the slope and look back you see how substantial it is, and how deftly it is integrated into the hillside, freeing most of the estate for a succession of green terraces. The concrete, mixed with local minerals, was poured into serrated moulds and chipped, then planted with creepers and flowers, so that it provides an easy transition between artfully arranged boulders and the greenery.

This was the first house that allowed Barba to fully test his ideas on bioclimatic architecture, and it brought him international recognition and several important commissions. It was designed for a creative couple with small daughters; two years later they sold it to the present owners, a family with four children, who invited the architect to complete the landscaping, and applaud the success of the experiment. Living underground is no novelty—there are troglodyte villages all around the Mediterranean;

the challenge was to create a house that exploited the insulating properties of the earth but felt comfortable and open.

The 220-square-metre house succeeds on both counts. Three bedrooms to the right of the entry and living areas to the left are rotated 45 degrees so that their windows face south; solid walls block the westerly sun. To achieve strength and exclude damp, the massive concrete walls have a ventilated cavity and a thin masonry lining, which is covered with painted plaster; the coffered concrete slab roof has two layers of PVC damp-proofing, and a sandwich of Catalan tiles and sand beneath the layer of soil, which is efficiently drained. The thermal mass of the ground keeps the interior cool in summer, and the double-glazed windows can be shaded from direct sun by horizontal shutters and a canvas awning that extends over the living room terrace. Windows and doors can be opened for natural ventilation, drawing in cool breezes off the sea. In winter the shutters are raised during the day and lowered at night, allowing the floor to absorb and retain the heat of the low sun. This passive solar gain is supplemented by electric ceiling heating in all rooms—the cost of which is one third of what it would be in a conventional house on this site. The earth also shields the occupants from the noise of traffic on a busy road. The garden descends beyond the house, and steps lead down to a pool.

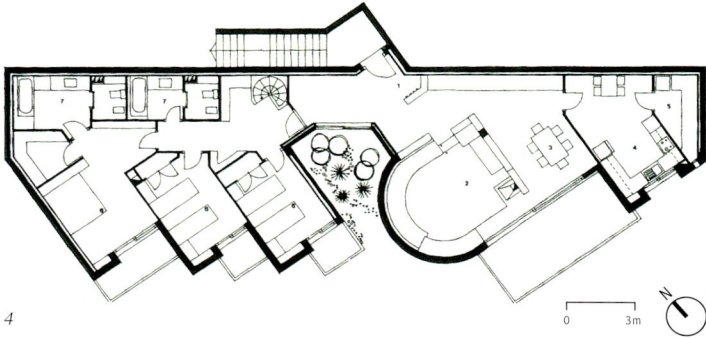
4

1 View from southwest
2 Sunken entrance
3 Rugged walls complement natural boulders
4 Plan
5 Landscaped roof terrace
6 Kitchen and canopied terrace
7 Entrance drive
8 Looking down on pool

5

6

7

8

9

10

11

12

9   Bedrooms
10   Link between sleeping and living zones
11   Kitchen and living area terrace
12   Living room

CARALPS HOUSE

Alella, Spain
Design/Completion 1989/1990

A well-known heart surgeon and his wife decided to move from Barcelona and build a new house on a 600-square-metre plot with a distant view of the sea, located near the tiny village of Alella. To accommodate the couple, their son and two daughters on so small a site, Barba designed a two-storey house with a hand-chipped concrete facade similar to that of Llavaneras. On the street side, the windows are small to reduce traffic noise, and the house opens up through picture windows to the southwest. The perimeter of the flat roof is planted, and the garage is sheltered by earth. The ground-floor living area has a Catalan tile floor and is divided into a small zone with a hearth for winter, and a larger space that opens to the garden in summer. There is a separate dining room, with kitchen and servants' quarters beyond. A skylit spiral stair leads to the upstairs bedrooms.

Opposite:
  Living room terrace

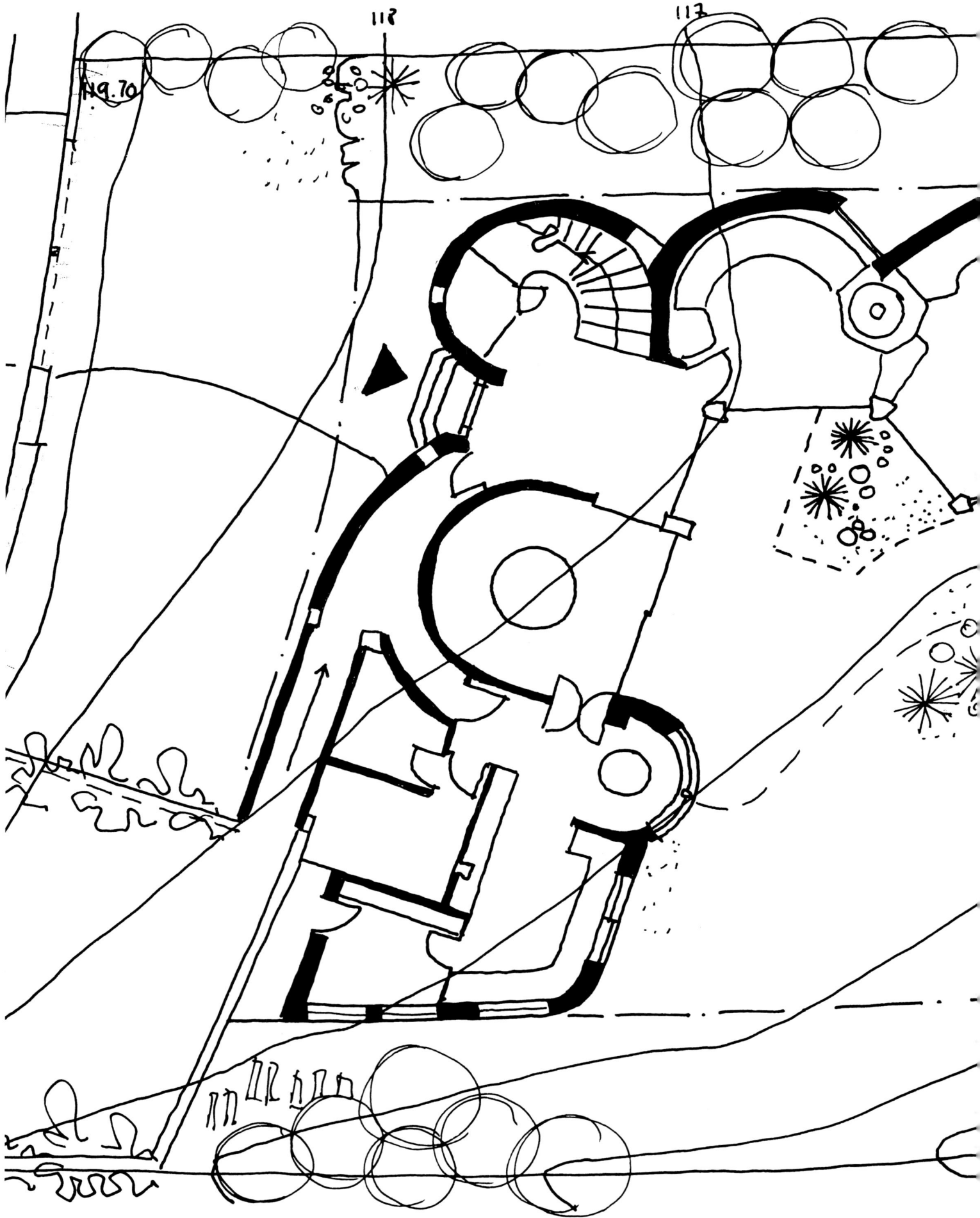

fig. 70

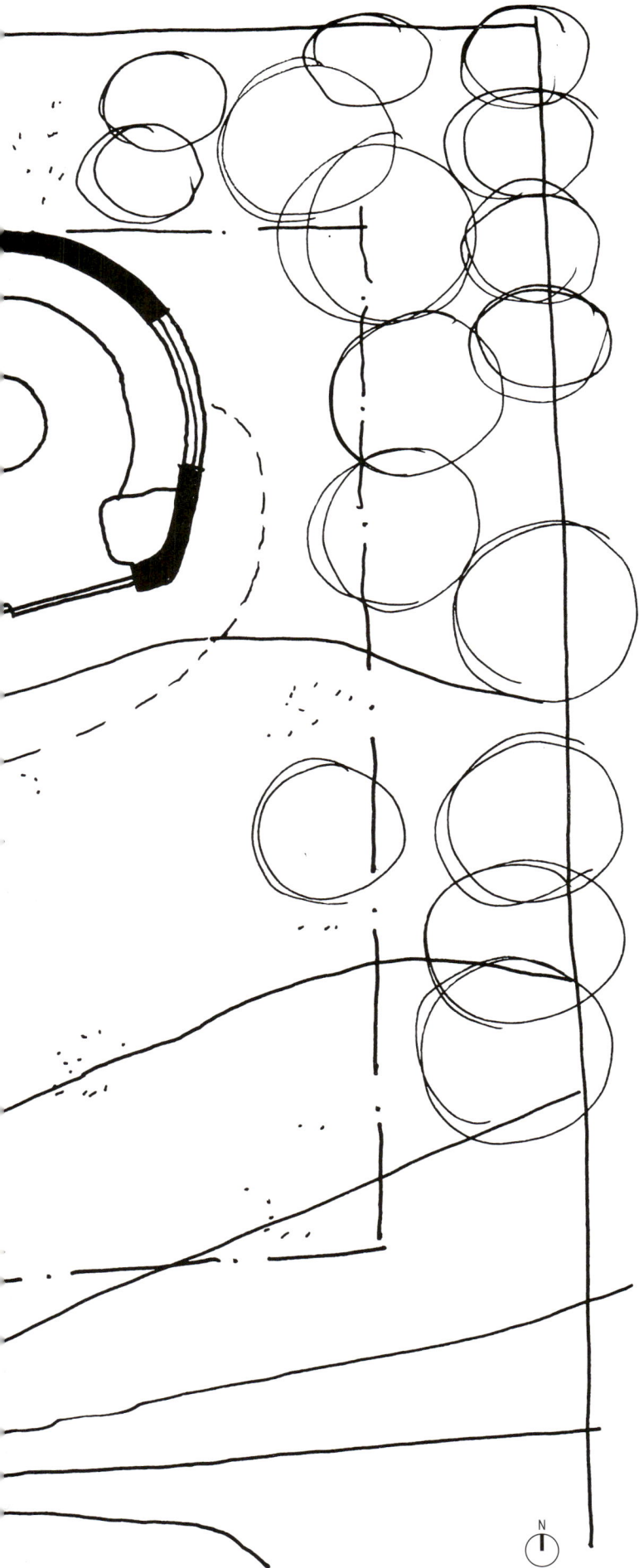

2   Plan
3   Bedroom (top floor); living area (bottom floor)

5

Previous page:
  Living room terrace
5   Entrance facade

7

8

GARATE HOUSE

Bonesvalls, Spain
Design/Completion 1990/1992

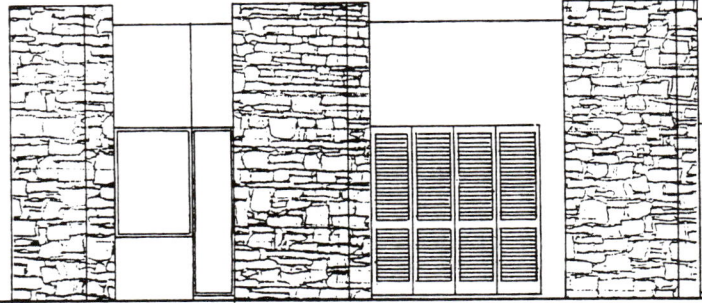

2

1

This 420-square-metre weekend house was built for a couple (he is Spanish, she is Swedish) who have, since their children grew up and left, lived here year-round. It extends along a grassy stone-buttressed terrace between a narrow upper road and the main road below, looking south over slopes planted with vines. The entry hall separates living from sleeping zones; from the front door you look out through full glazing to the garden. Steps lead down to a media room beneath the garage. The living room is contained within a stone-faced cut-away cylinder, from which a wide circular canopy projects to shade the paved terrace. A spiral stair leads up to a mezzanine study which opens onto the concrete slab of the canopy, which is treated as a pebbled roof terrace bordered by planters. The dining room is contained within a smaller stone

Continued...

1   *Entrance*
2   *Front facade*
3   *Bedrooms and living room at night*

3

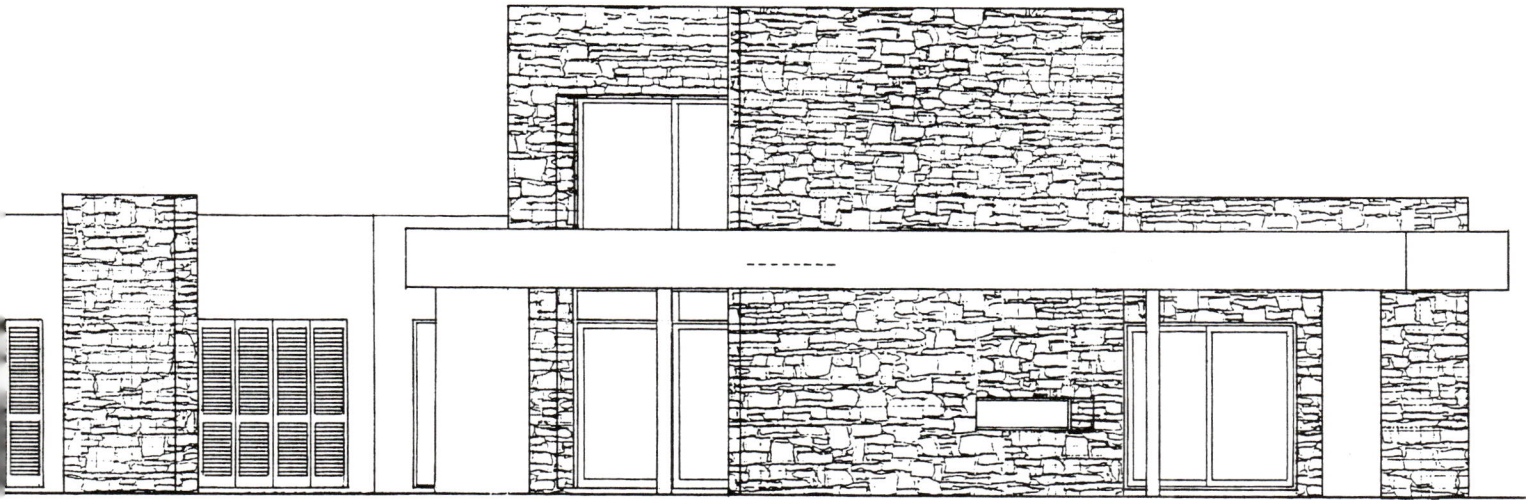

4

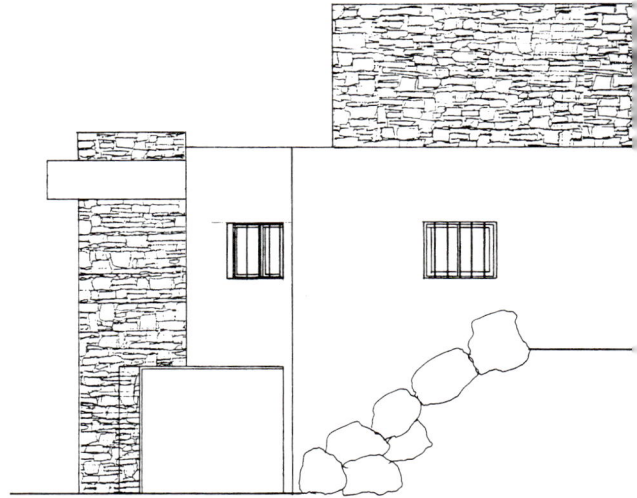

5

6

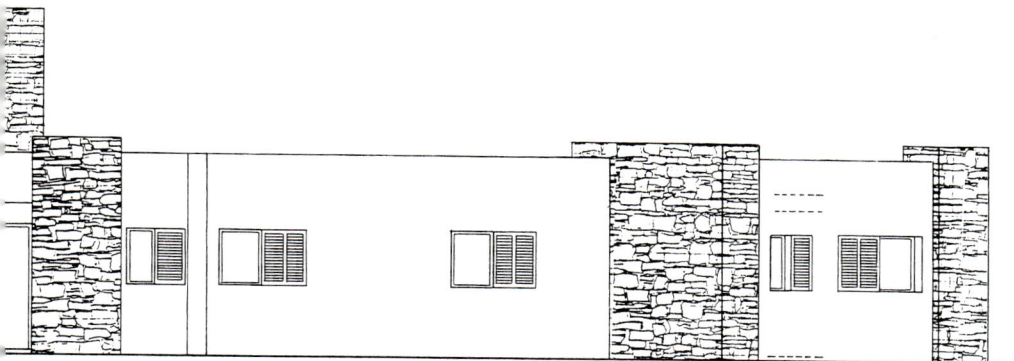

cylinder, opening into the living room and kitchen. Extending from this cluster is a row of three bedrooms on a saw-tooth plan, each opening out onto lawn, and linked by a skylit corridor. At the far end of the terrace is a pool house which doubles as an informal dining pavilion.

Barba has made masterly use of simple geometries and complementary materials. The curved walls are clad with stone that is laid with the artistry of the Anasazi ruins in Chaco Canyon, New Mexico. The concrete of the canopy and bedroom walls is exposed and coloured a soft ochre. The intersecting circles play off each other and the angles of the bedroom wing. That's all there is, and it is all that's needed. The modest interiors have quarry tiled floors and stylish contemporary furniture and light fittings, accented by a few heirlooms.

4   Roof terrace
5   Back facade and entrance
6   Bedrooms (left), living and study (right) from garden

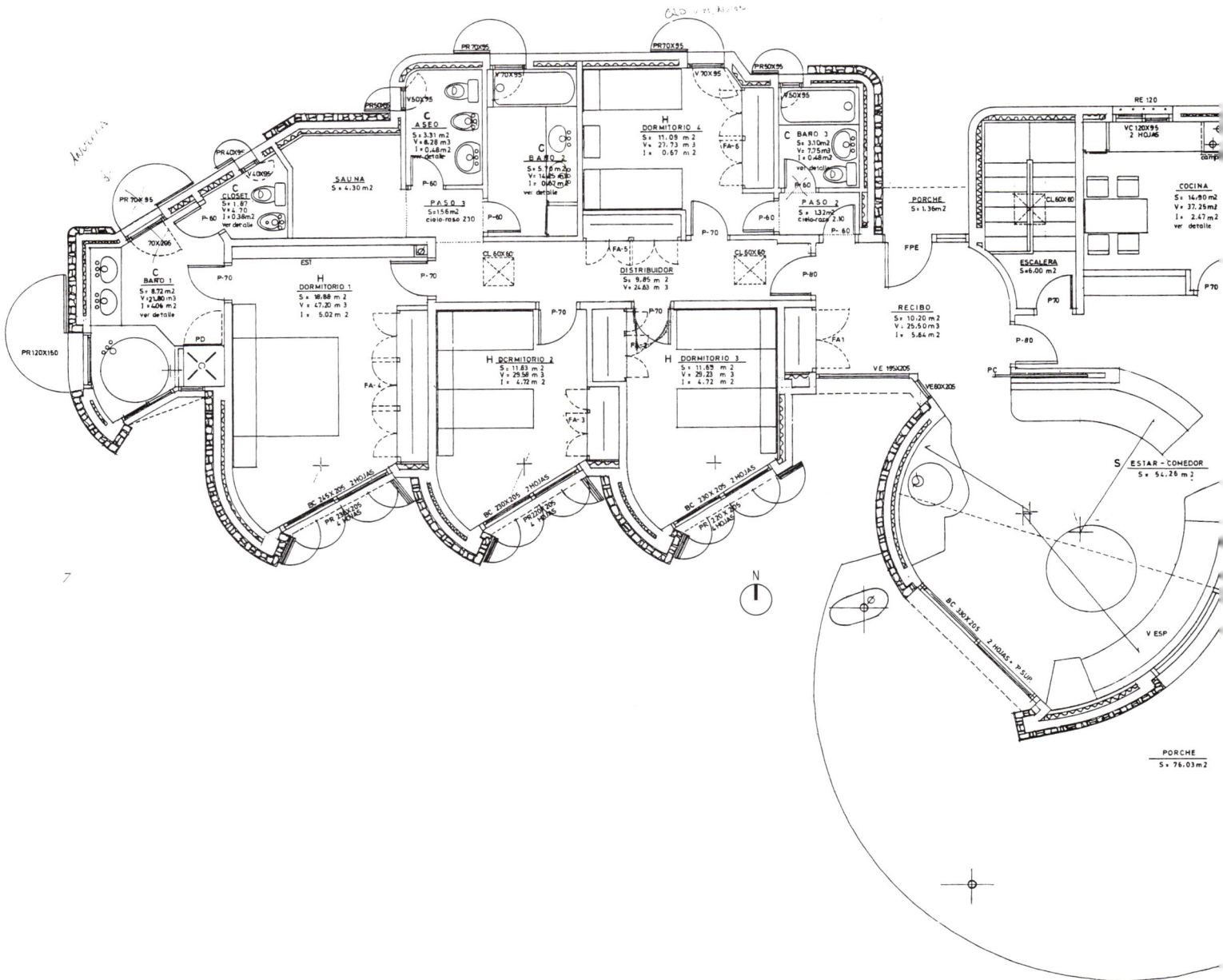

Plan annotations (floor plan):

RE 120
VC 120X95
2 HOJAS

PR 70X95
V 70X95
PR 70X95
PR 50X95
V 50X95

ASEO
S= 3.31 m2
V= 8.28 m3
I= 0.48 m2
ver detalle

BAÑO 2
S= 5.78 m2
V= 14.45 m3
I= 0.82 m2
ver detalle

DORMITORIO 4
S= 11.09 m2
V= 27.73 m3
I= 0.67 m2

BAÑO 3
S= 3.10 m2
V= 7.75 m3
I= 0.48 m2

COCINA
S= 14.90 m2
V= 37.25 m3
I= 2.47 m2
ver detalle

SAUNA
S= 4.30 m2

CLOSET
S= 1.87
V= 4.70
ver detalle

PASO 3
cielo-raso 2.10

PORCHE
S= 1.36 m2

ESCALERA
S= 6.00 m2

BAÑO 1
S= 8.72 m2
V= 21.80 m3
I= 4.06 m2
ver detalle

DORMITORIO 1
S= 16.88 m2
V= 47.20 m3
I= 5.02 m2

PASO 2
cielo-raso 2.10

DISTRIBUIDOR
S= 9.85 m2
V= 24.63 m3

RECIBO
S= 10.20 m2
V= 25.50 m3
I= 5.84 m2

DORMITORIO 2
S= 11.83 m2
V= 29.58 m3
I= 4.72 m2

DORMITORIO 3
S= 11.65 m2
V= 29.23 m3
I= 4.72 m2

ESTAR - COMEDOR
S= 54.26 m2

PORCHE
S= 76.03 m2

N

7 Plan
8&9 Living room terrace
10 West facade of living room and terrace
11 Rear facade of living room and lower level garage
12 Living room terrace

8

9

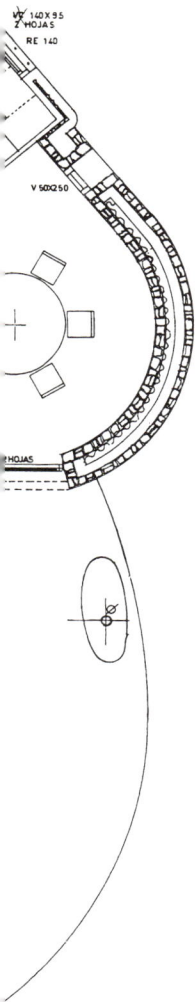

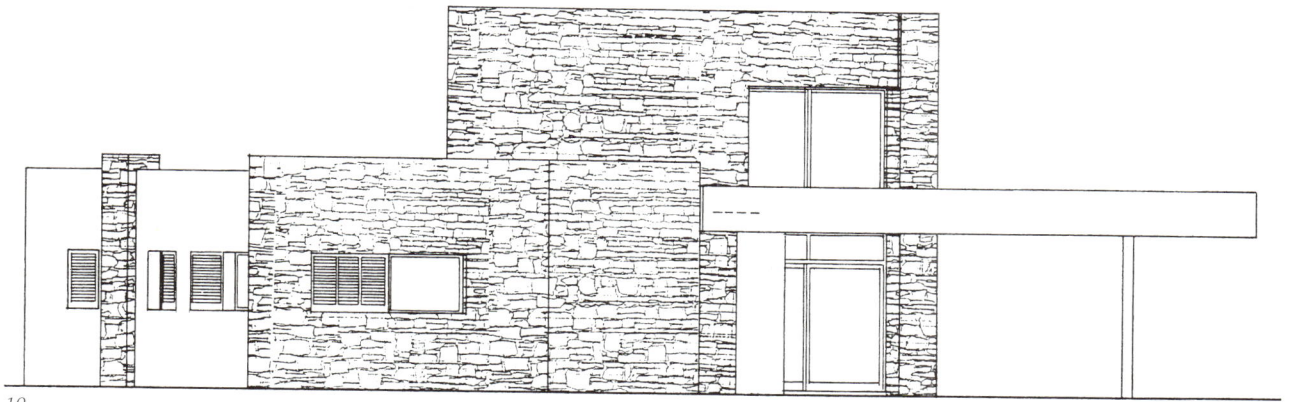

10

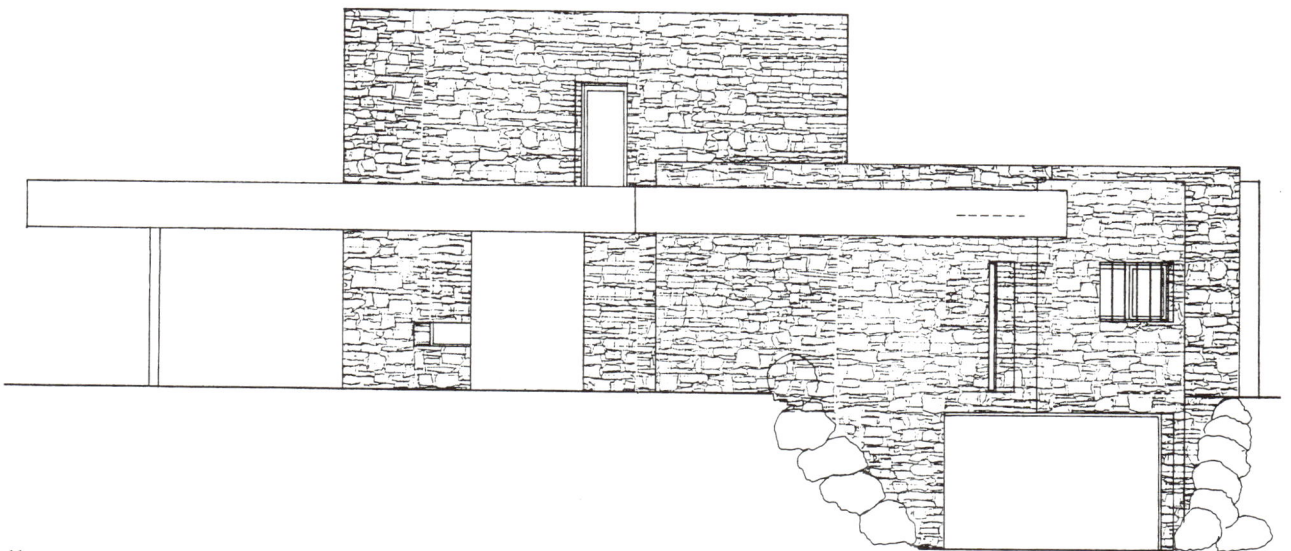

11

12

13

14

15

16

17

18

19

20

21

22

23

18–23 *General views and details of the living room*

25

26

27

Opposite & 25
Dining room
26&27   Master bathroom

MONJO HOUSE

Menorca, Spain
Design/Completion 1990/1991

1

Commissioned to build a summer house for
a large Spanish family, Barba lived on the site
for two weeks, sleeping with Pamela on the floor
of a farmhouse on the next promontory, and
sketching in the sand. As a dedicated mineral
collector, he briefly considered adding a pyramid
of red glass that would glow like a ruby from the
rock. 'If I build this, I am going to be famous!,'
he thought, but he quickly rejected the idea. The
rock-bound cove with its pure sand and amethyst
sea was one of the great unspoilt treasures of the
Mediterranean, and he understood that the
house should defer to the towering rocks against
which it was to be set.

Barba removed an unsightly viewing platform,
retained an old square stone tower (which would
be remodelled to contain children's bedrooms)
and designed a sequence of canted stone-clad
concrete walls enclosing living spaces that
emerge from the rock, with a flat roof that is
landscaped with local wildflowers and ice plants.
The roof becomes another terrace in the garden,
and the living areas open onto a paved pool
terrace overlooking the beach. Windows face
east and buttresses offer protection from the
fierce August sun—which is when the house
is most used. The parents sleep in a separate
structure, and there is a guest house further
up the slope.

Continued...

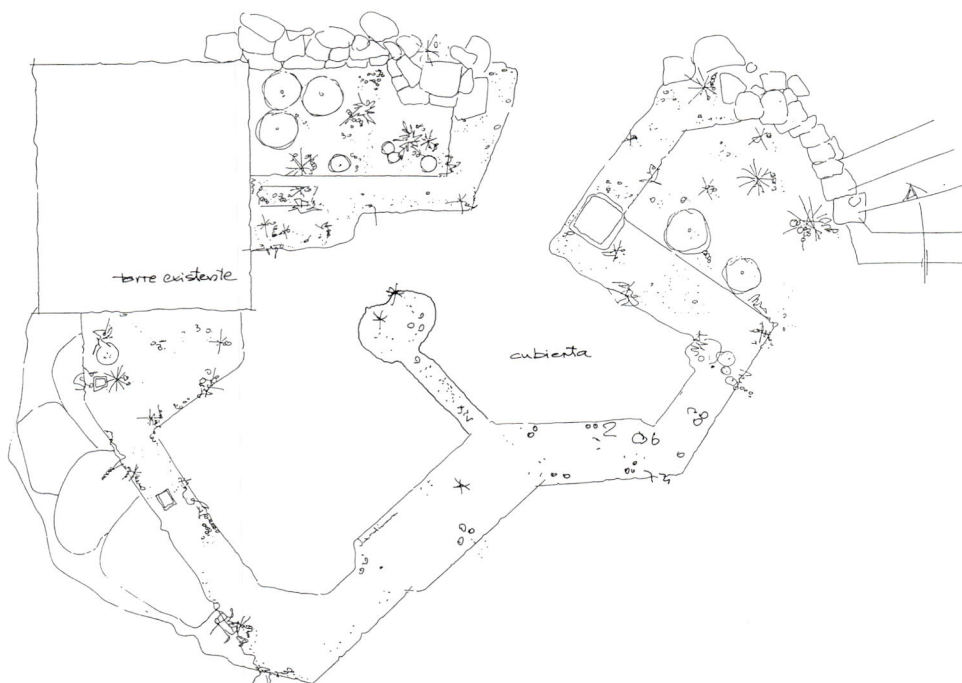

2

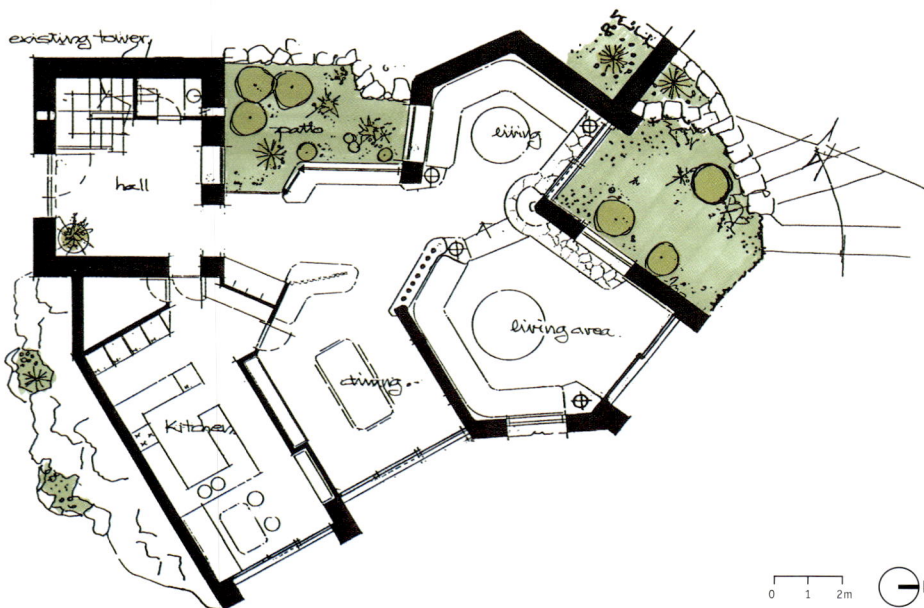

1   *House from across cove*
2   *Landscape plan*
3   *Floor plan*
Opposite:
   House from below

3

6

7

Previous pages:
House and pool
6 Landscaped roof terrace
7 Guest pavilion

8

9

The design clearly owes a debt to Mesa Verde (the Anasazi ruin in Colorado), and to the stone megaliths of ancient settlers who inhabited the caves of Menorca; it contrasts sharply with the whitewashed geometry of the local vernacular—an example of which occupies the base of the hill. From a distance, the buildings disappear into the craggy hillside. An enclosed court brings light into the heart of the house and provides cross-ventilation. The simple interiors draw on that vernacular, with their clay tiled floors, stone-clad or whitewashed walls, traditional doors and pierced confessional screens. The furniture is sparse: solid wood tables and chairs, and a built-in sofa, for the lucky owners spend most of their waking hours outside.

10

11

8   *Living area*
9   *Main living area*
10   *Dining area of guest house*
11   *Guest house living area*

GIRO SUMMER PAVILION

Sitges, Spain
Design/Completion 1995/1996

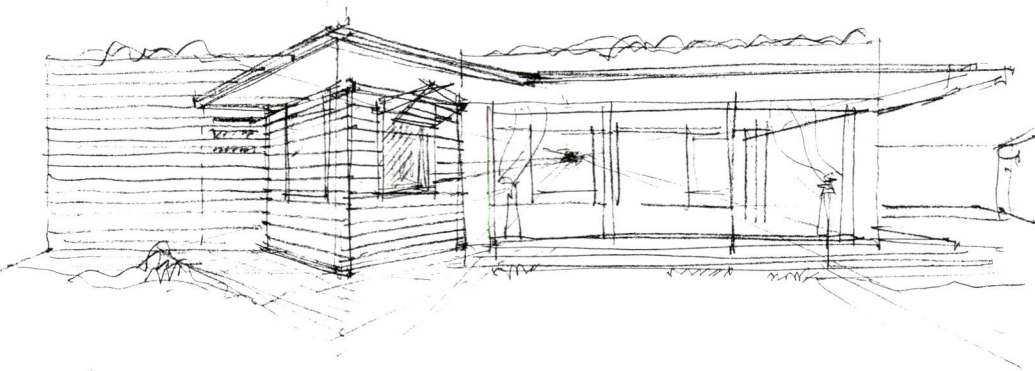

1

2

Sitges is a dignified old seaside resort a few kilometres to the west of Barcelona, and it has held at bay the tawdry commercialism that has disfigured much of the coast. Like Biarritz, it seems caught in a time warp, and the ornate mansions that may once have lodged English milords and Russian grand dukes have survived to accommodate a new generation of pleasure-seekers. A young couple bought such a house and commissioned Barba to create a pool in the exquisitely manicured garden. They also needed a convenient place to change, and this modest program mutated into one of the architect's most delightful miniatures: a low, rectangular pavilion that opens up through glass walls to a slatted deck that is wrapped around the L-plan pool.

The pavilion serves as an informal complement to the house, and one that expresses the barefoot, outdoor routine of summer in which one changes, bathes, enjoys a light lunch, and takes an afternoon nap in the same place. Any shack would provide the essential shelter, but Barba has done more, scaling the pavilion to house and pool, adding frescoes to give the dining room a distinctive character, and landscaping the flat roof to unite it with the garden. Also enclosed is a small kitchen, a sitting area, and showers.

1   Sketch
2   Changing area
Opposite:
    Pavilion and pool at night

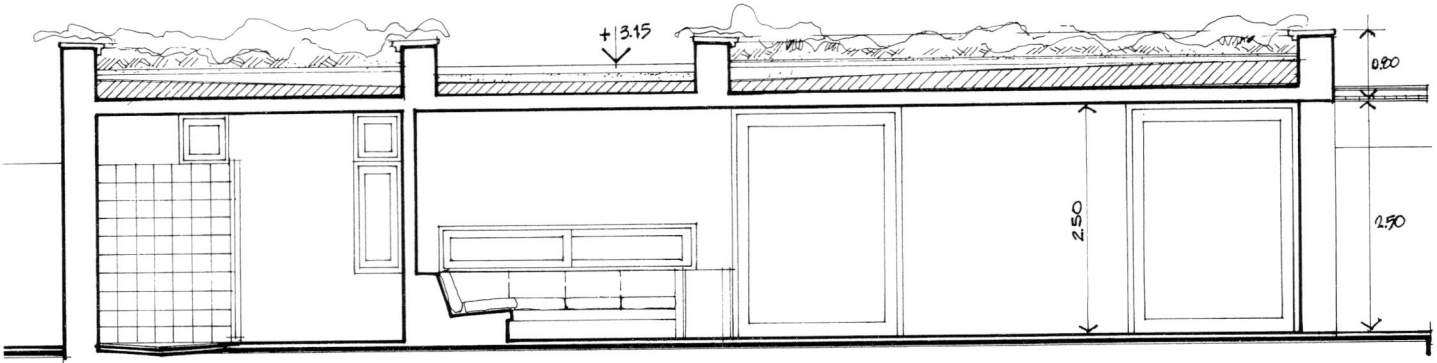

+ 3.15

0.90

2.50

2.50

5

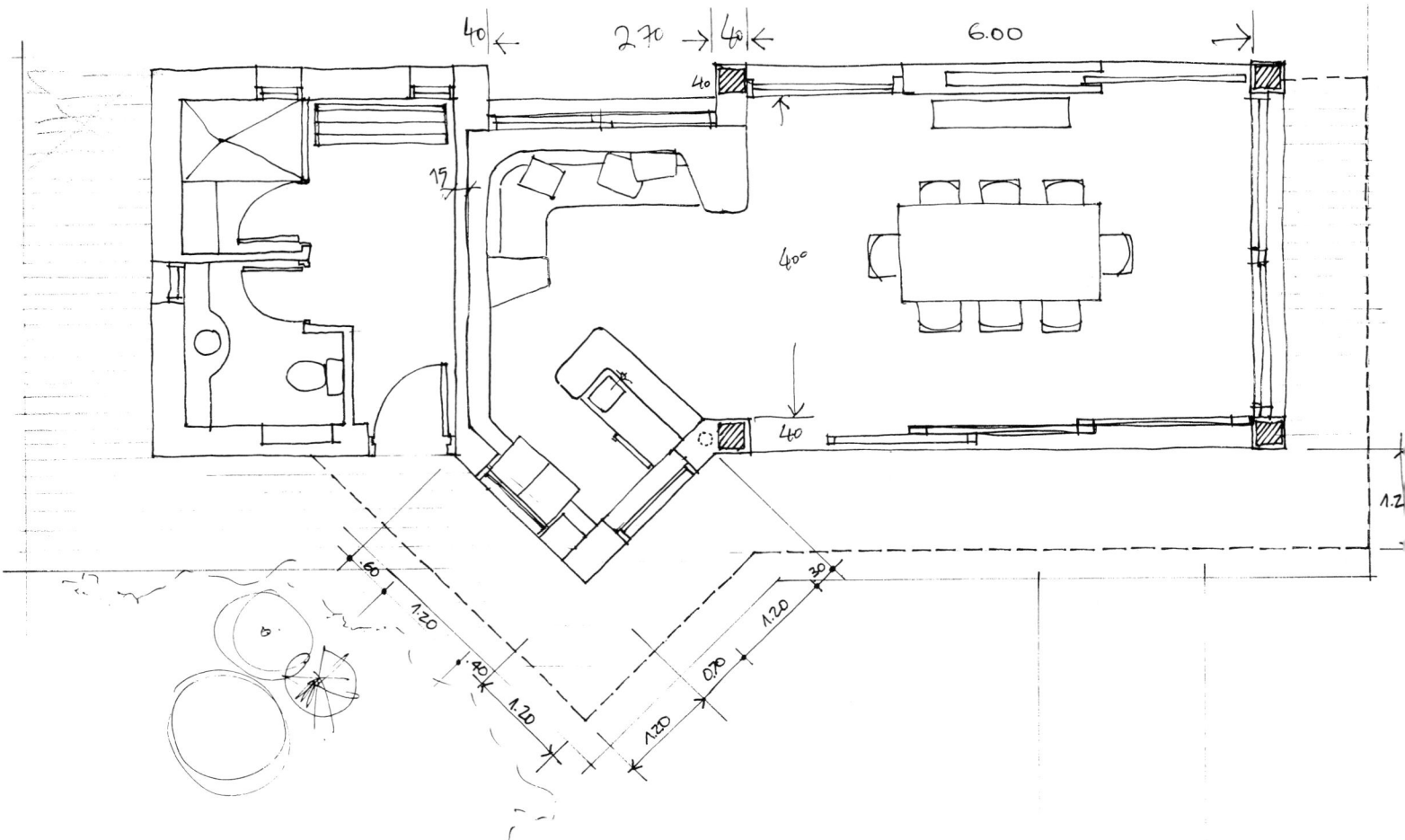

40

2.70

40

6.00

40

15

400

40

.60

1.20

40

1.20

1.20

30

0.70

1.20

1.20

1.2

6

7

8

9

10

11

9   Dining room
10   Sitting area
11   Bathroom

MORA HOUSE (1)

Calella de Palafrugell, Spain
Design/Completion 1991/1992

1

Barba is lucky enough to find clients who trust him. Once he has developed an understanding of their personalities and needs, and how they plan to use the house, he presents them with alternatives, making models to demonstrate how the parts fit together. But here, the client—an old friend from school-days—shrugged and suggested the architect should do whatever he thought best. The product of that decision evolved out of the Bonesvalls' house, deploying similar stone and coloured concrete forms in a binuclear plan, with the entry hall as a hinge.

However, there are some interesting variations on the original theme.

The house is located in fields; a four-minute drive from the bustling coastline, but a world away in spirit. A ramshackle farmhouse that occupied the site was demolished, but it finds an echo in the rough pink stone work and barn-like interior of the two-storey bedroom wing. In contrast, the stacked stones that clad the living areas outside and in, have a refined quality. The main spaces are low and hexagonal, unlike the tall cylinder

of the Garate house. Its floors are of polished slate, the ceiling of rough plaster, and there is a steel firehood that was designed by the architect's father. The projecting circular canopy with its roof garden for insulation is much wider, defining an outdoor room that surrounds the enclosed area on two sides and is separated from it by a stone parapet and windows. Barba would have liked to cantilever the roof plane, but decided to support it on pipe columns, which also serve to drain the roof garden.

1   Old house and new

2

3

2   Living room
3   View from pool

4

5

6

7

4   Kitchen
5   Dining room
6   Section
7   Hall linking sleeping and living areas

8

8   Living room

9

10

9   Master bedroom
10   Master bathroom

ROTHSCHILD
SUMMER PAVILION

Corfu, Greece
Design/Completion 1993/1994

The concept for this commission was similar to that of Giro in Sitges—a summer pavilion and pool to complement an existing house—but on a much larger scale, for the client was Lord Jacob Rothschild, a patron of architecture whose family underwrote the construction of the new Supreme Court of Israel in Jerusalem, and the site was a spectacular headland on Corfu, looking across the water to Albania. He had rejected proposals by five leading architects over a period of six years, but, when he saw an *Architectural Digest* feature on the Menorcan house, he decided to invite Barba to London, and, after a long conversation, offered him the job.

Continued...

1 View of site
2 Rendering of site

3

Lord Rothschild was concerned to preserve the natural beauty of the headland, and Barba discovered an ideal location—a long-concealed Venetian marble quarry. He cleaned it out, extracted some stone, and used its rough sides as a natural backdrop for the huge overflow pool, and the pavilion—which was inspired by the villas that rich Romans built on sites like this. Warm stucco arches frame the covered pool, and an open-sided white pergola shelters sitting and dining areas, with a kitchen, changing rooms and bathrooms beyond. Classical statues and reliefs, and a Byzantine mosaic are incorporated into the new construction; the site has been enhanced with stone-walled terraces and an antique fountain, and planted with olives and cypresses under the supervision of Lord Rothschild's daughter, Beth. Off to one side, Emmy Rothschild designed an imposing entrance in the guise of a ruin, with stone columns and a skeletal roof, reinforcing the impression that these buildings are refurbished survivors from antiquity. The clients were delighted. 'Javier's great contribution was his feeling for the site—how, in uncovering its essence, he made such wonderful use of it,' said Lord Rothschild of Barba's work. 'He has created an Arcadia.'

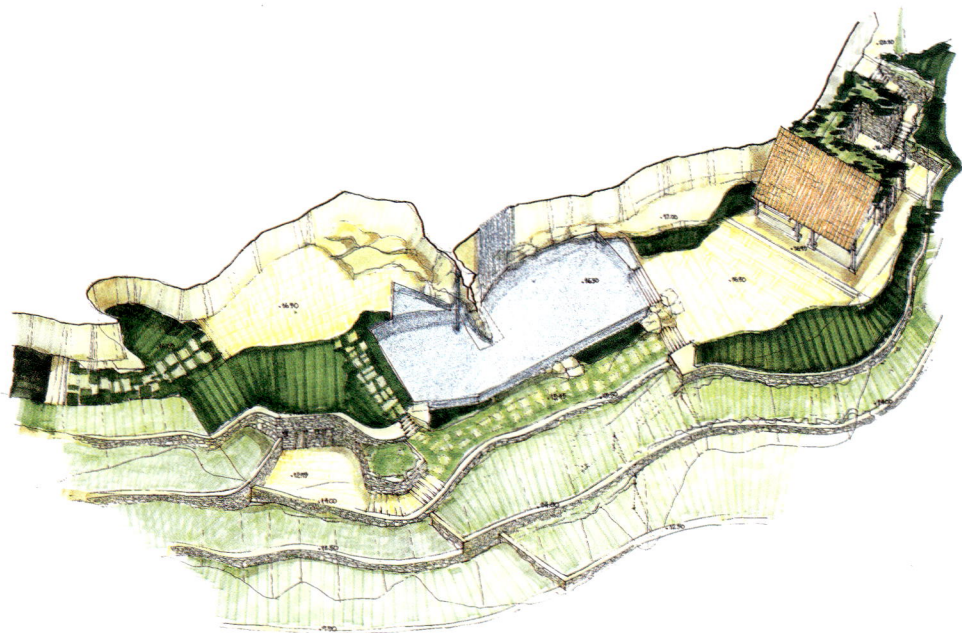

3   Pavilion and pool
4   Landscape plan
Following pages:
5   Pool
6   View from canopied shade area

4

5

6

8

9

10

11

13

TSIRIGAKIS HOUSE

Mykonos, Greece
Design/Completion 1997/1998

1

An Athenian couple—he is in shipping and she edits a fashion magazine—with one young son wanted a weekend retreat on the rugged uplands of Mykonos, far from the tourist hordes in the port, which would capture the unchanging beauty of the island. The risk of earthquakes mandated reinforced concrete construction, and the house had to be protected from the fierce winds that sweep the Aegean. Walls extend to shelter the pool and embrace the stepped entrance court. To root the building in the landscape and reduce maintenance,

Continued...

1   Protective wall
2   North facade
Below:
     Roof detail

5

6

Barba has clad most of the surfaces in local rock, making only limited use of the smooth whitewashed stucco of the Greek island vernacular, which he believes is more appropriate for houses that are clustered together than for a stand-alone. As with the house on Menorca, the new construction fades into the rockscape and drystone walls from a distance, leaving the few sensuously rounded white walls, a cupola over the shower, and distinctive white chimneys to evoke an isolated farmhouse, and accentuate the angularity of the exposed masonry. A traditional canopy of logs and woven twigs supported on stone piers shades a terrace that overlooks the harbour.

Continued...

Opposite:
Bedroom (left); master bathroom (centre & right)
5   *Main entrance to patio, north facade*
6   *Stone and stucco*

7

8

7   Roof detail
8   Entrance patio, detail of lizard mosiac

The 200-square-metre interior comprises a living-dining area, master suite and three guest bedrooms on the main floor, and a two-bedroom apartment for the son and guests below. It is built around a rock outcrop that was once the home of a lizard—now the subject of a mosaic in the forecourt. Natural light softly illuminates the interior, with its rounded white walls, arches and columns, traditional wood beam ceilings, and maple-strip floors. The junction of walls and floors is marked by rope, reminding the owner of his maritime associations, and old doors and mirrors are incorporated within the new decor. Steps and a low wall divide the dining area from the living room, which is elegantly furnished with Christian Liaigre chairs and sofas. The master bathroom has a vaulted plunge pool inspired by those of antiquity, and two rough-sided rock bowls to serve as basins. This is a house in which every detail puts one in touch with nature, and where one can glimpse the full moon from one's bed or in the bath.

9

10

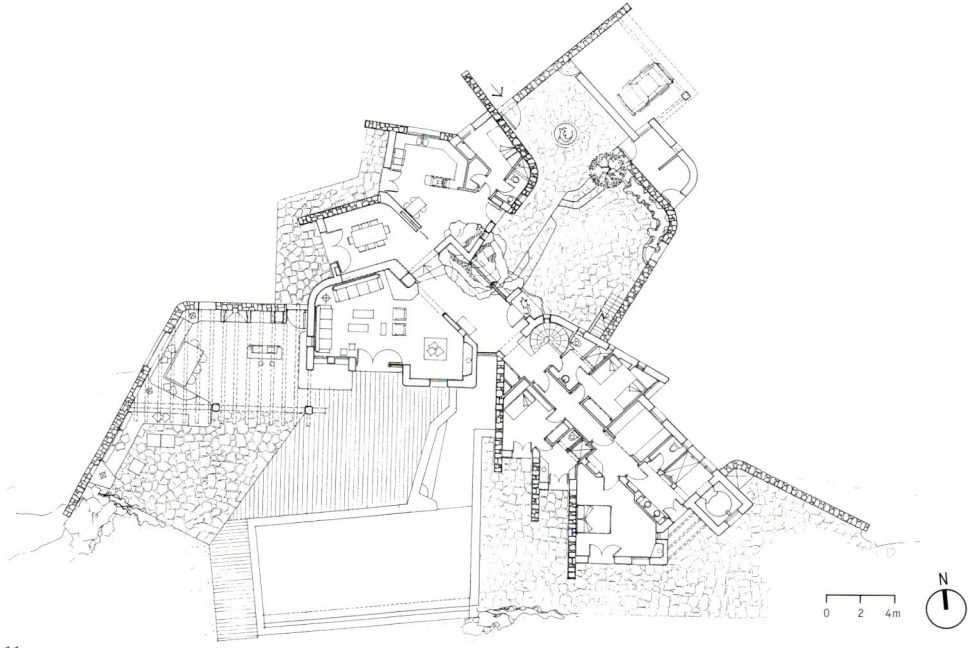

11

12

13

14

13　Perspective sketch of main entrance (left) and kitchen (right)
14　Living room
15　Lizard carved in stone
16　Living room
17　Detail of old wooden door

15

16

17

18

18   Master bedroom
19   Master bathroom has vaulted plunge pool

19

MORA HOUSE (2)

Llafranch, Spain
Design/Completion 1997/1998

A couple who are good friends of the architect and residents of Barcelona wanted a weekend-summer house for themselves and their two small and two grown children. In contrast to his brother in Calella, the client picked a constrained but elevated lot at the heart of this small seaside town, looking out to a spectacular rocky cove. To accommodate 460 square metres of covered space within the mandatory setbacks and height limit was a challenge that Barba solved by creating his first cubist house—a tight-knit complex of interlocking volumes on two levels. The living and service spaces occupy the ground floor and open onto a side patio and to a pool that looks south towards the coastline. Upstairs bedrooms have access to terraces, a landscaped roof, and upper belvedere. There is an underground garage for four cars and a boat.

Barba has known the Mora's since they were at school together, and he enjoyed his client's trust. To reduce the impact of this large house

Continued...

1

2

4

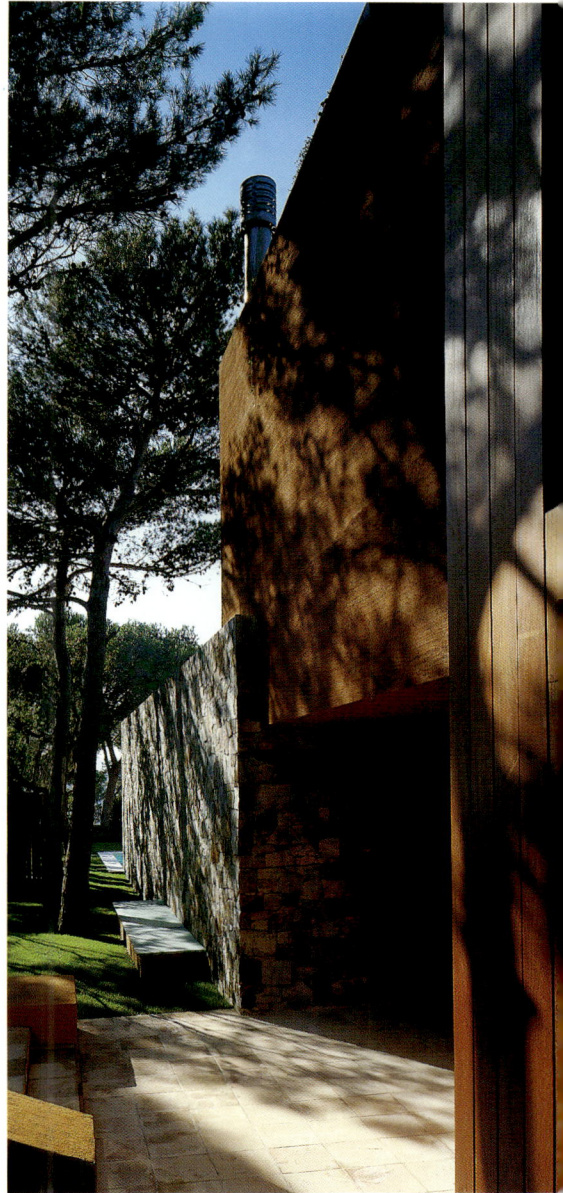
5

1   Entrance
2   Street facade
Opposite:
    Pool terrace
4   Street front detail
5   Street facade

on the neighbourhood, he has employed oxidized stone for a screen wall that shuts out traffic noise and the prevailing wind, two tones of ochre concrete that pick up on the colour of the stone, and wood siding—similar materials to those that make his country houses merge into the landscape. The restrained palette and sheer walls give the house a pleasing sense of solidity. A pergola and canvas awning provide shade, and motorized louvres in the wood siding open up like fish gills to admit or exclude light.

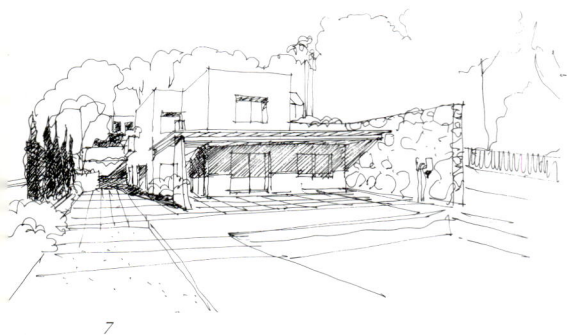

7

8

9

Previous pages:
View from southwest
7–9 *Perspective sketches*
Opposite:
From southwest at night

11

12

11 Kitchen
12 Bathroom

VAN VEGGEL HOUSE

Cascais, Portugal
Design/Completion 1998/1999

1

2

3

Mr. van Veggel, a young Dutch executive who moved to Portugal to direct a company that constructs commercial centres and office complexes, bought a mountaintop site on the edge of a national forest with a distant view of the Atlantic, a half-hour commute from Lisbon. He and his wife saw pictures of the Rothschild Pavilion, and asked Barba to build them a house that would respond to the natural beauty of the 6,000-square-metre triangular plot. They also wanted it to be designed according to the principles of *feng shui*; happily, Barba and an Italian student working in his office were familiar with these.

Architect and client made and exchanged collages of images of features that might inspire the design, including cobbled courtyards, ornate arches, walls covered with *azulejos*, and bougainvillea spilling over white stucco.

For Barba, this was a way of starting a dialogue and discovering his client's likes and dislikes. His plans evolved from these discussions, making use of local materials and elements from the local vernacular, but abstracting them. Construction is of reinforced concrete to withstand earthquakes The high-walled entrance courtyard with its geometric paving is enriched by aromatic plants and the sound of a waterfall. A canopy shelters the entrance from rain, and pergolas are wrapped around the south side. Stone-flagged living areas are built over the lower-level garage and service rooms, and they fan out like the fingers of a hand to command the view of forest and ocean to the north. Triple glazing and wooden louvres offer protection from summer sun. Bedrooms extend out to the southwest and northwest.

1   Model
2&3 Sketch
4   Upper level plan
5&6 Entrance to small living area (left) which
     connects to larger living area (right)
7   Master bedroom
8   Master bathroom
9   Sunken bath connected to master bedroom

4

0 2.5 5m

N

5

6

7

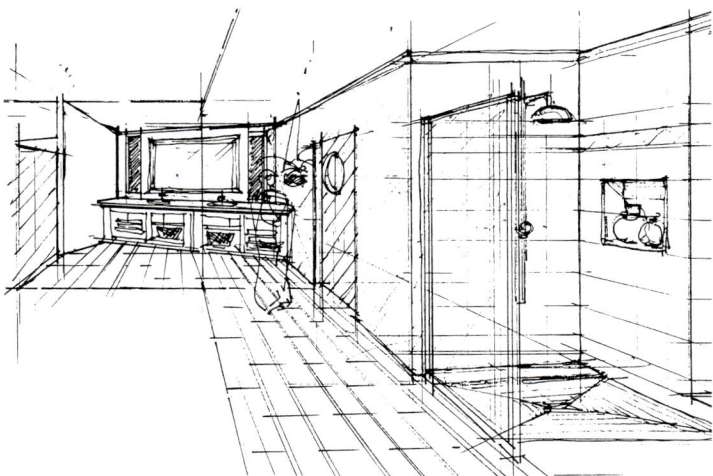

8

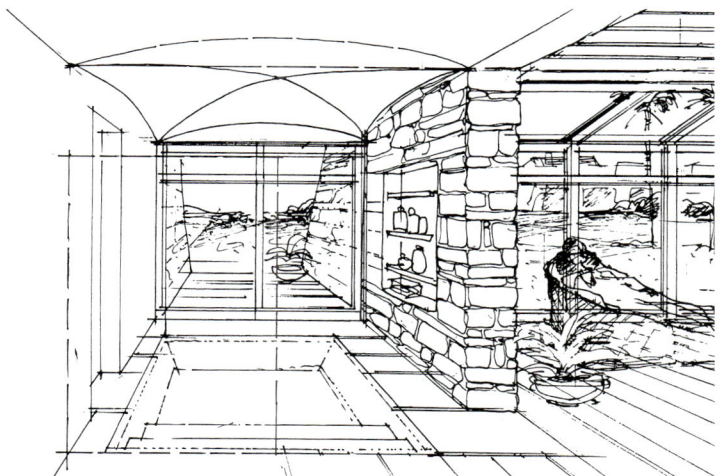

9

LUXURY RESORT PROJECT

Borobudur, Indonesia
Design 1993/not constructed

The landscape of central Java, with its lush vegetation, terraced rice paddies, and mountains, provides an ideal setting for one of the wonders of the world: the 1,100-year-old Buddhist temple of Borobudur, a UNESCO World Heritage site that resembles a ziggurat of carved stone figures. Barba was invited to create a luxury hotel on a hillside overlooking the temple and decided that he would take his cues from the topography and the vernacular. The 50 guest bungalows were nestled into the contours of the land, making them invisible from above, and the public facilities at the top of the slope were designed as *Pendopos*—traditional open-sided timber structures, comprising roofs supported on columns.

Guests will enter through a patio walled with the same basaltic black stone that was used for the temple, and enter the lobby, which leads to the separate structures housing the common rooms, bars, and restaurant. The lobby will be reflected in a pool, and the water will circulate to other pools and falls around the site. Each bungalow will have an unimpeded view of the temple, and have its own garden, pool, and outdoor sleeping area that will be sheltered from the views of others. This exciting project has yet to be realized but the concept inspired Barba's plans for a resort in Baja California.

2

3

1

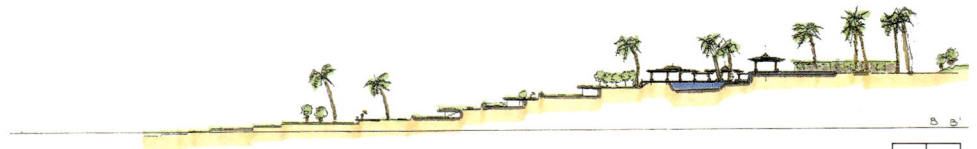

4

5

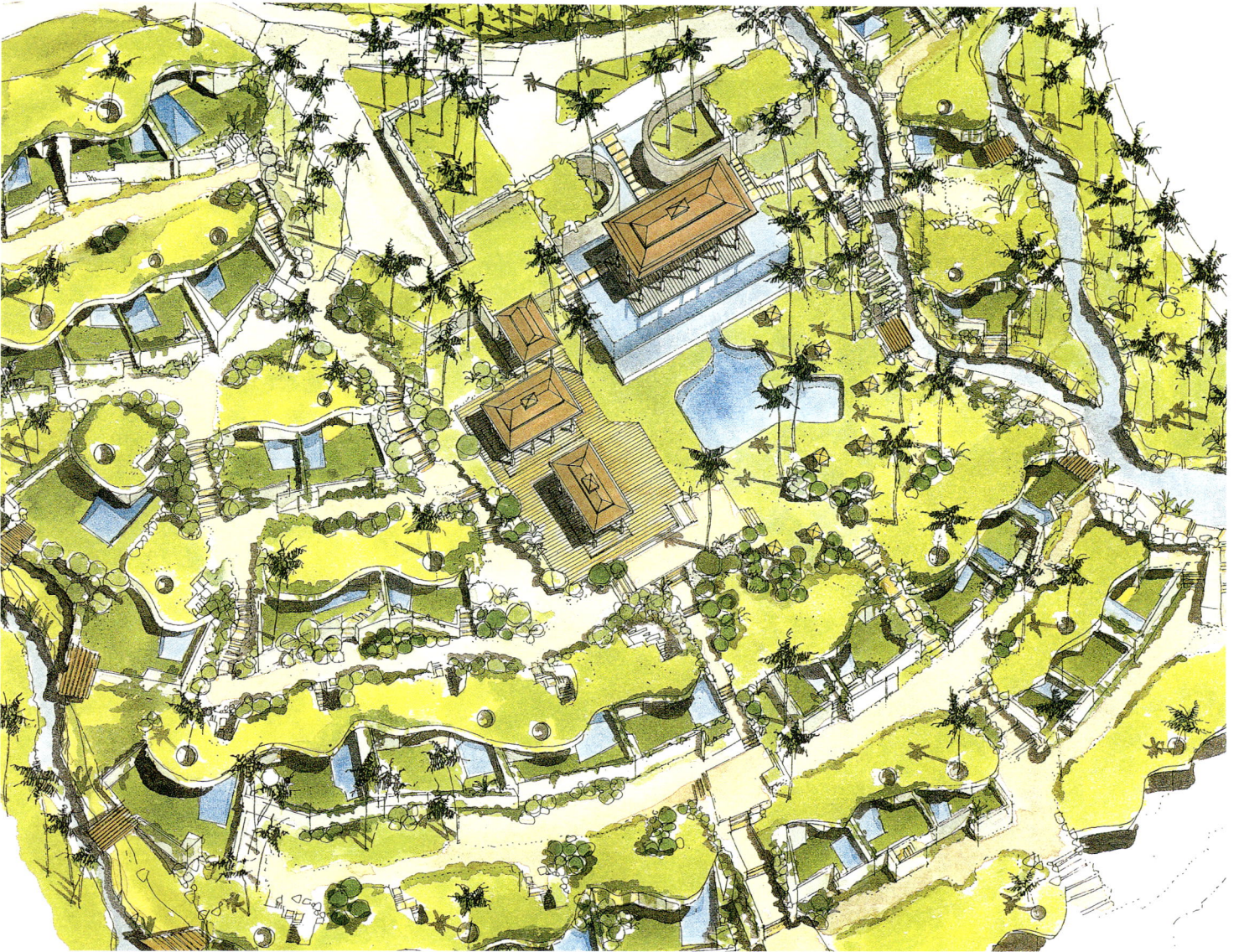

6

1   Proposed idea for bungalow entrance
2&6   Renderings of project
3–5   Sections

GREEN ISLAND
PROJECT

Barcelona, Spain
Design 1992/not constructed

When the 1992 summer Olympics were awarded to Barcelona, the city authorities seized the opportunity (and generous state funding) to make major urban improvements—most notably to redevelop the waterfront. Marinas, a broad pedestrian promenade, and a high-rise hotel–office complex have replaced what was formerly a decayed industrial zone. Barba proposed an audacious scheme: to bring the best of the Costa Brava to the city by constructing a green island, 40 metres offshore, linked by a causeway to the beach. The plan was to create two artificial hills, containing 202-earth-sheltered, solar-powered apartments for couples and small families, which would also shelter an 800-boat marina. Restaurants, bars and shops would occupy the bottom rim, and a parking garage would be housed within the hills. The entire outer surface would be thickly planted with oaks and pines so that, from shore or sea construction would be concealed and the island would appear to be wild. This ecologically sustainable community attracted wide popular support and serious interest from Japanese investors, and, though it was not built in Barcelona, there is strong interest from overseas developers.

1

2

3

4

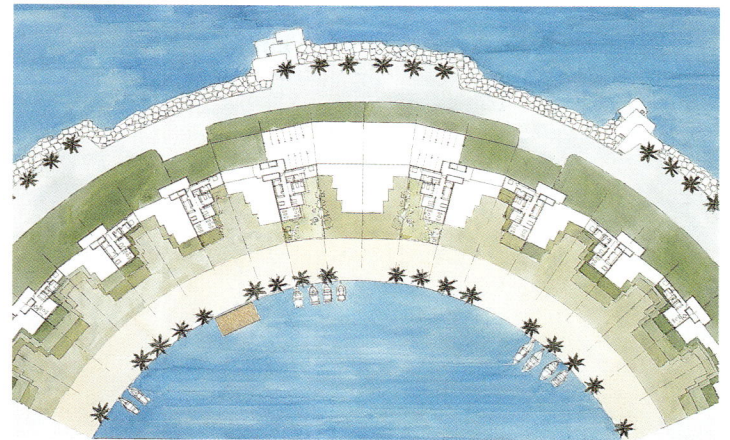

5

6

7

8

9

1 Simulated aerial view
2 Rendering
3 Section
4 Bridge, main entrance to island
5 Apartment floor plan
6 Port entrance
7 Overall view
8 Port
9 Rendering

10

11

12

13

12&13   Model of Green Island

PUNTA SAN BASILIO RESORT

Baja California Sur, Mexico
Design 1996—

This is a project that Barba hopes will vindicate his ideas for ecologically responsible residential architecture on a large scale. He was first approached in 1990 by Paul Cote, a Canadian financier and founder-member of Greenpeace, to develop a concept for a resort community on a wild site in Baja California. They met, discussed ideas, but the project languished. Then, in 1996 Cote invited Barba to meet him and new partners on an even more spectacular, 800-hectare expanse of inlets, unspoilt beaches, jutting rocks and desert. He flew to Loreto, camped beside the beach, and—too excited to sleep—walked around by the light of a full moon. Over breakfast, the developers asked him what he would do. 'The site is so gorgeous, I propose to do nothing,' he replied. 'We've found our architect!' they exclaimed, and Barba began sketching.

Over the past two years, the plans have been developed for a mix of stone and adobe buildings, a botanical garden and lagoon, and 90 one- and two-bedroom cottages with private pools, in addition to a marina, fishing village, and a country club with desert golf course. The hotel complex derives directly from the proposal for Borobudur, abstracting vernacular buildings for the public spaces, and concealing guest accommodations in a hillside with landscaped roofs, much like the Riera house in Llavaneras, 15 years earlier. All the buildings will employ local materials and traditional colours, textures and furnishings. But they will also harness the latest technologies to generate solar power and recycle water, and will provide electric cars for transportation within the site. Even the lighting will be concealed so that guests will be able to look up at night and enjoy a celestial dome of stars.

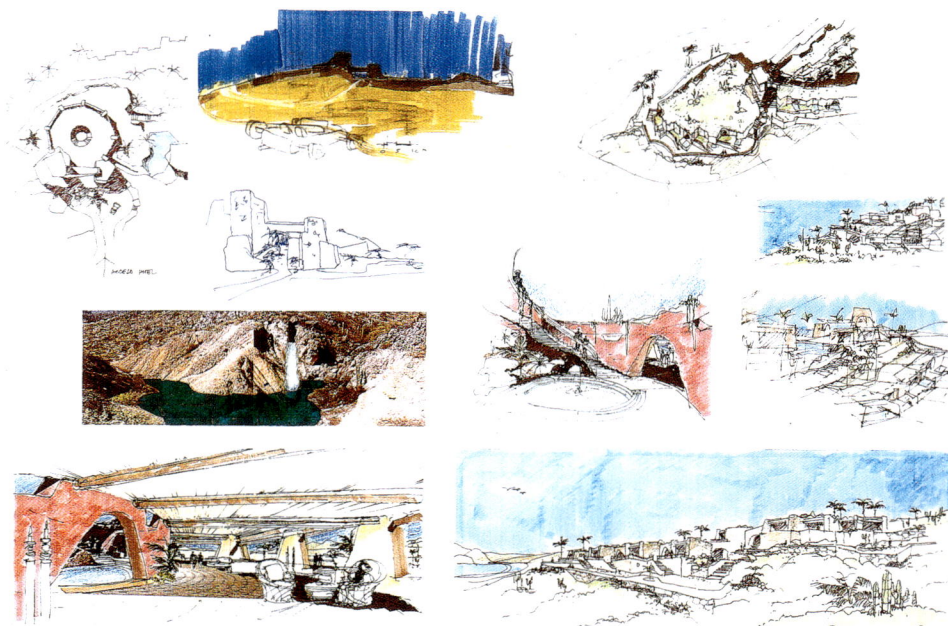

1

2

3

4

TERRAZA PANORÁMICA HALL

RESTAURANTE BAR

ZONA SERVICIO

APARTAMENTOS JUNIOR

JUNIORS ZONA ALTA

APARTAMENTOS SENIOR

ZONA DEPORTIVA

ÁREA PISCINAS

CAPILLA

VIALES

5

1–3   Sketches of resort
4   Zoning Plan
5   Site plan

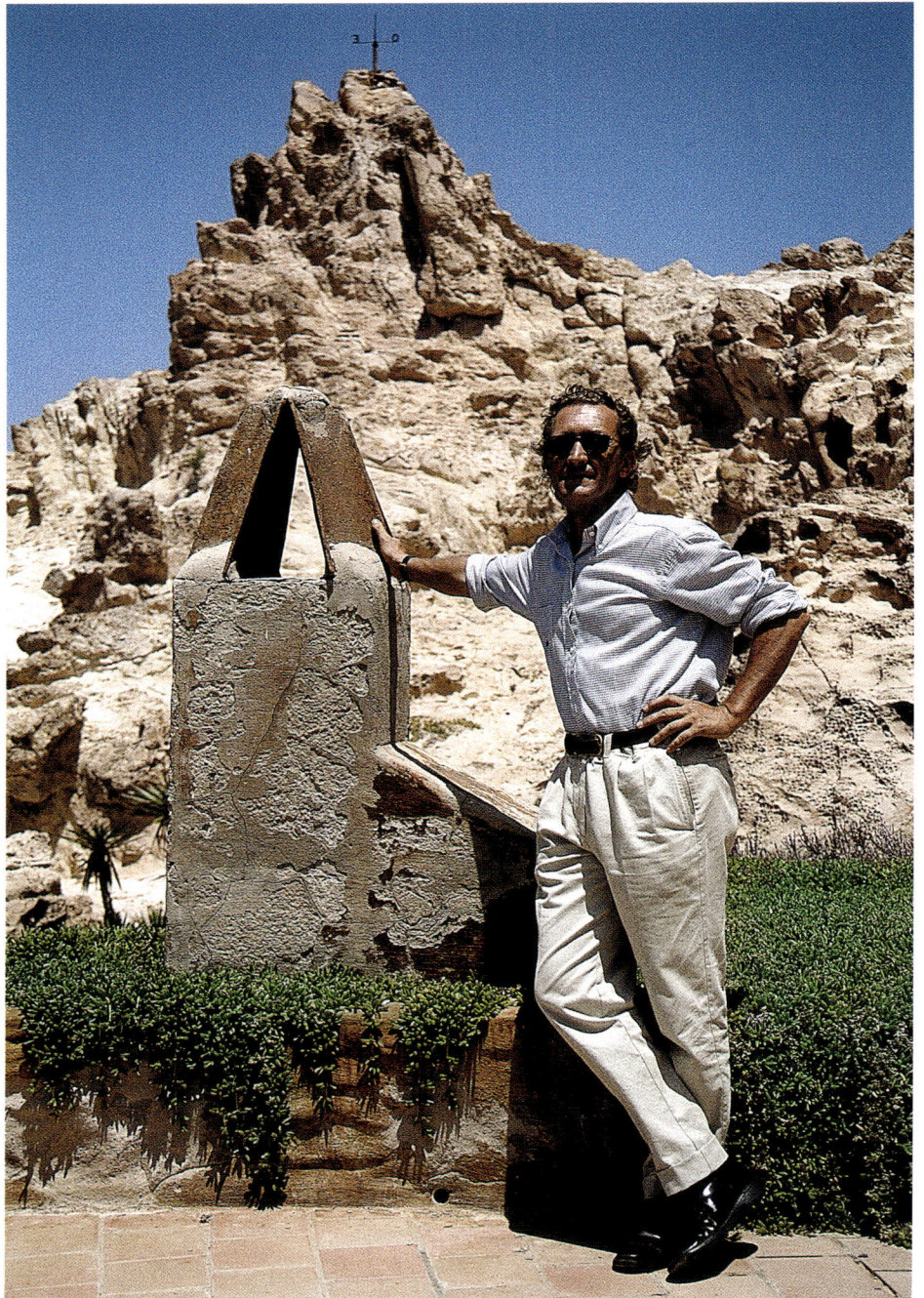

Javier Barba was born in Barcelona, Spain in 1948. The son and grandson of architects, Javier grew up immersed in the world of architecture. After graduating from secondary school, Barba did not doubt his choice of careers and enrolled in the Barcelona School of Architecture in 1967.

In 1972 he joined his father´s firm, where he gained experience but yearned for a different type of architecture, breaking off from the rationalist tradition of Le Corbusier and feeling more inspired by Frank Lloyd Wright. His development as an architect came from his work; each building was in itself an experiment and an evolution, leading to the next so that one can see a progression of forms, with his master being the natural environment itself. In 1980 he formed his own practice, Estudio BC. In a time of mass production of impersonal buildings, Barba has been faithful to the idea of 'haute couture'

instead of 'prêt a porter' architecture, fitting each site with a building appropriate to its characteristics. Recognized as one of the leaders of the Green Movement of Integrated Architecture, Barba has lectured at home at the University of Barcelona and the University of Seville, and abroad at the Ben Gurion University in Israel, at the Congress on Sustainable Architecture in Crete, at the International Congress on Sustainability and at the University of Monterrey Mexico.

In 1989 the Commission of the European Community chose the Llavaneras semi-buried house to feature in Project Monitor as an example of one of the best bioclimatic constructions in Europe. In 1993 Barba contributed an article on Integrated Bioclimatic Architecture to the George Wright Forum and has been invited to participitate in international competitions amongst which was the

Cathedral of St Vibiana in Los Angeles. Barba´s work has been published in many international magazines and has been featured on the covers of several. Currently, Barba is living in Barcelona when not travelling to far ends of the globe to work on his growing number of commissions.

SELECTED BIBLIOGRAPHY

Architectural Digest (USA), January 1987, Earth Sheltered House, Spain, pp 90–95.

Architectural Digest (USA), January 1988, Earth Sheltered House, Spain, pp 58–65.

Architectural Digest (USA), January 1992, Menorcan House, Spain, Cover & pp 96–101.

Architectural Digest (USA), May 1992, Menorcan House, Spain, pp 62–67.

Architectural Digest (USA), September 1992, Earth Sheltered House, Spain, p 48.

Architectural Digest (Italy), 1992, Menorcan House, Spain.

Architectural Digest (USA), September 1995, One Hundred Best Architects and Designers, p 28.

Architectural Digest (USA), October 1995, Rothschild House, Corfu, Greece, pp 210–218.

Architectural Digest (Germany), February 1997, Corfu House, Greece.

Architectural Digest (Germany), April 1998, Menorcan House, Spain.

Architectural Digest (USA), January 1999, Mykonos House, Greece.

Architectural Record (USA), August 1992, Earth Sheltered House, Spain, p 53.

Architecture and Design (Japan), 1992, Earth Sheltered House, Spain, p 16.

Arquitectura Bioclimática (Spain), 1989, Earth Sheltered House, Spain, pp 25–28.

Atlantico (Spain), 13 October 1995, Arquitectura Verde, Spain, p 6.

Avui (Spain), 9 June 1992, Alella House, Spain.

Avui (Spain), 7 May 1995, Menorcan House, Spain.

Avui (Spain), Vilanova, Santiago, 1995, Art and Ecology, Spain, (30 May).

Baño y Cocina (Spain), January 1995, Olesa House, Spain, pp 36–40.

Barcelona Divina (Spain), 1995, Green Island Project, Spain, No 4.

Bartolucci, Marisa 1995, Architecture for a Small Planet, *Town and Country* (USA), (September), p 76.

Boletin Agropecuario (Spain) 1995, p42.

Business Seminar, Green Island Project/Borobudur Project/Menorcan House/Earth Sheltered House, Spain.

Casa Campo (Spain), March 1994, Earth Sheltered House, Spain, pp 46–55.

Casa Oggi (Italy), July 1992, Menorcan House, Spain, Cover & pp 50–57.

Casa Vogue (Spain), July 1992, Menorcan House, Spain, pp 70–75.

CIC Información (Spain), November 1992, Earth Sheltered House/Menorcan House, Spain, pp 53 & 54.

Conference in Verona, Italy, October 1995, Ecological Construction.

Conference in Vigo, Spain, October 1995.

Country Houses, 1991, Earth Sheltered House, Spain, pp. 89–96.

Diario 16 (Spain), 13 October 1995, Arquitectura Ecologica, p 11.

Eficiencia Energética (Spain), November 1992, Earth Sheltered House, Spain, pp 6 & 7.

Eficiencia Energética (Spain), February 1993, Earth Sheltered House, Spain, p 12.

El Correo Gallego (Spain), 13 October 1995, Arquitectura Verde, p12.

El Mueble (Spain), July 1995, Pool–Calella House, Spain, p 110.

El Pais (Spain), 14 January 1996, Arquitectura de padre a hijo.

El Pais, 2 August 1998, Corfu House, Greece.

El Pais (Spain), 16 August 1998, Mykonos House, Greece.

El Periodico (Spain), 8 July 1995, Green Island Project, Spain, p 30.

El Punt (Spain), 8 May 1995, Artists for Nature.

Emiti (Greece), June 1994, Earth Sheltered House/Green Island Project, pp 153–158.

Emiti (Greece), December 1994, Menorcan House, Spain pp 151, 156, 160.

Exposition, Miro Museum, Spain, 1996, Homo Ecologicus, Green Island Project, Spain.

Faro de Vigo (Spain), 13 October 1995, De Cara Almar, p 4.

Forum 1993, Spain, Earth Sheltered House/Menorcan House/Borobudur Project/Green Island Project, pp 59–71.

Guell, Xavier 1986, Earth Sheltered House, *Casas Mediterraneas*, (Barcelona, Spain: Gustavo Gili).

Hogares (Spain), November 1992, Alella House, Spain, pp 78–87.

Houses by the Sea, 1991, Menorcan House, (Spain: Editorial Atrium), Cover & pp 28–37.

Impermeabilización (Spain), 1992, Earth Sheltered House/Menorcan House, Spain, pp 4–9.

Impermeabilización Professional (Spain), July 1992, Underground Sports Facility (Sotaverd), Spain, pp 36–41.

Impermeabilización Professional (Spain), April 1995, Green Island Project, Spain, pp 39 & 40.

Interior Design, 1989, Earth Sheltered House, Spain (Spain: Editorial Atrium), pp 44–49.

La Casa (Spain), 1993, p 39.

La Vanguardia (Spain), 1985, Earth Sheltered House, Spain.

La Vanguardia (Spain), 27 March 1994, Green Island Project, Spain.

La Vanguardia (Spain), 24 March 1996, Corfu House, Greece.

La Vanguardia (Spain), 22 September 1996, Olesa House, Spain.

La Vanguardia (Spain), 26 November 1996, Arquitectura en la cuna de los dioses, p 94.

La Voz de Vigo (Spain), 13 October 1995, Abrir Vigo al Mar.

Mackenzie, Dorothy 1991, Earth Sheltered House/Menorcan House, *Green Design*, (England: Laurence King Ltd), pp 10–12, 37–39, 66 & 67.

Madame (France), 1993, Menorcan House, Spain, pp 69–71.

Manual Guia Technica De Los Revestimientso y Pavimentos Ceramicos, Spain, 1988, p 180.

Metropolis (USA), January 1992, Earth Sheltered House/Menorcan House, Spain, p 47.

Nautic Press, May 1994, Green Island Project, Spain, p 5.

Raum and Wohnen (Germany), August 1992, Menorcan House, Spain, p 80–90.

Seminar on Bioclimatic Architecture, Cyprus, 1994.

Vale, Brenda & Robert 1991, Earth Sheltered House, *Green Architecture*, (England: Thames & Hudson), Cover & pp 146 & 147.

Vila Olimpica (Spain), August 1995, Ecological Island, Spain, Cover.

Ville Giardini (Italy), July 1993, Earth Sheltered House, Spain, pp 32–37.

World Residential Design, 1991, Earth Sheltered House, (Japan: The Moriyama Editors Studio), pp 17–22.

In publishing this work The Images Publishing Group Pty Ltd recognizes that despite the best efforts of all concerned this bibliography is not a complete listing.

CHRONOLOGICAL LIST OF BUILDINGS AND PROJECTS

* Denotes projects featured in this publication

1975–1980

(Projects in collaboration with architect Francisco Juan Barba Corsini)

1980–82

99 apartments—Soldeu, Andorra
(in collaboration with Neil Minto and Juan Ramón Mora)

1982–83

12 apartments—Anyos, Andorra
(in collaboration with Juan Ramón Mora and Juan Ignacio Canela)

1983–84

3 speculation houses—Turo dén Llull, Llavaneras, Spain
(in collaboration with Javier Perez del Pulgar)

1985–86

Commercial Center—Galerías Boulevard Borbón—36 shop mall, Barcelona, Spain
(in collaboration with Alfredo Vives)

Jover/Riera House, Llavaneras, Spain

1985–87

Perez del Pulgar House, Bellaterra, Spain

Project for a village in Binisafua, Menorca, Spain
(in collaboration with Alfredo Vives)

1987–88

27 semi-attached houses, Vallpineda, Sitges, Spain
(in collaboration with Estudio L-35 Arquitects)

Project for Hotel Centro Termal de Talasoterapia, Sitges, Spain
(in collaboration with Alfredo Vives)

1988–90

Palacios House, Sant Cugat del Vallés, Spain
(in collaboration with Enrique López de Manresa and Carlos del Saz)

1989–1990

*Caralps House, Alella, Spain
(in collaboration with Lorenzo Barbón)

1990–92

*Garate House, Olesa de Bonesvalls, Spain
(in collaboration with Enrique López de Manresa and Carlos del Saz)

*Monjo House, Menorca, Spain
(in collaboration with Alfredo Vives)

1990–93

Sports Center, Piscinas y Deportes (35,000 m² underground construction), Barcelona, Spain
(in collaboration with L-35 Arquitects)

1991–92

Allary House, Llavaneras, Spain

*Mora House (1), Calella, Spain
(in collaboration with Alfredo Vives)

1991–93

18 bioclimatic houses, Bollvir, Spain
(in collaboration with Alfredo Vives)

Apartment Block, Calle Bertan, Barcelona, Spain
(in collaboration with Enrique López de Manresa)

1992

Project for reform of Club Bonasport, Barcelona, Spain

1992/not constructed

*Green Island Project, Barcelona, Spain
(in collaboration with Alfredo Vives and Susana Zanon)

1993/not constructed

*Luxury Resort Project, Borobudur, Java, Indonesia
(in collaboration with Alfredo Vives and Susana Zanon)

1993

Project Sports Club, Vilasar de Mar, Spain

1993/1994

*Rothschild Summer Pavilion, Corfu, Greece
(in collaboration with Alfredo Vives and Susana Zanon)

1994

Ecovillage, Sanillés, Spain
(in collaboration with Susana Zanon)

Project for Bioclimatic Building in Jaffa Israel...Catalan/Israeli
(in collaboration with Orlando de Urrutia)

Project for Rothschild Gate House, Corfu, Greece
(in collaboration with Susana Zanon)

1995

Rubert de Ventós House, Sant Martí de Ampurias, Spain
(in collaboration with Susana Zanon)

1995–96

*Giro Summer Pavilion, Sitges, Spain
(in collaboration with Susana Zanon)

1996–

*Punta San Basilio Resort, Baja California Sur, Mexico
(in collaboration with Alfredo Vives and Susana Zanon)

1996

Landscape Pool Project, Robert Ryan Ranch, Montana, USA
(in collaboration with Susana Zanon)

1996–1998

Beunza House, Javea, Spain
(in collaboration with Susana Zanon)

1997

Almada Shopping Center, Lisbon, Portugal
(in collaboration with Alfredo Vives and Susana Zanon)

Beach Club and Beach Houses, Punta San Basilio, Baja California, Mexico
(in collaboration with Susana Zanon)

Commercial Center, Oviedo, Spain
(in collaboration with Alfredo Vives and Susana Zanon)

Hotel Resort, San Martin de los Andes, Argentina
(in collaboration with Susana Zanon)

Planells—Golobart House, Santa Cristina D'Aro
(under construction)
(in collaboration with Susana Zanon)

1997/1998

*Mora House (2), Llafranch, Spain
(in collaboration with Susana Zanon)

*Tsirigakis House, Mykonos, Greece
(in collaboration with Susana Zanon)

1998

Pallejá-Salvat House, Valldoreix, Spain
(in collaboration with Susana Zanon)

Perez del Pulgar House, Bellaterra, Spain
(in collaboration with Susana Zanon)

Residential Aparment Complex, Soldeu, Andorra
(in collaboration with Susana Zanon)

Residential Complex, Sant Mori, Spain
(in collaboration with Susana Zanon)

Residential Complex (36 houses), Binisafua, Menorca, Spain
(in collaboration with Alfredo Vives and Fernando Pons)

Sanchez Vicario House, Sitges, Spain
(in collaboration with Susana Zanon)

Stag´s Leap Winery, Napa Valley, California, USA
(Winiarsky Family)
(in collaboration with Susana Zanon)

Swarovski Residence, Cala Pregonda, Menorca, Spain
(in collaboration with Susana Zanon)

Van Veggel Pool Project, Estoril, Spain

1998/1999

*Van Veggel House, Cascais (Lisbon), Portugal
(under construction)
(in collaboration with Susana Zanon)

INDEX

PHOTOGRAPHY CREDITS

Luis Casals: 10–13, 36–43, 44–47, 49–51

Emilio Rodriguez: 14, 15, 17–23, 24–35

Eugenio Pons: 52–62, 64–93

Javier Barba: 6, 96 (1), 98–105

Michael Webb: 106